The Art of the Woodland Indians

Decoration on pouch, Delaware, porcupine quills on deerskin, Denver Art Museum, photograph by Alfred Tamarin

Shirley Glubok

Designed by Gerard Nook · Special Photography by Alfred Tamarin

Macmillan Publishing Co., Inc.
New York
Collier Macmillan Publishers
London

The author gratefully acknowledges the assistance of:
Richard Conn, Curator of Native Arts, The Denver Art Museum; *Charles E. Gillette,* Curator of Archaeology, New York State Museum and Science Service; *Kathleen Bishop-Glover,* Assistant Curator of Collections, Canadian Ethnology Service; *Conrad E. W. Graham,* Assistant Registrar, McCord Museum; *Patty Harjo,* Conservateur, Denver Museum of Natural History; *Nancy Oestreich Lurie,* Curator of Anthropology, Milwaukee Public Museum; *Martha Potter Otto,* Head, Department of Archaeology, Ohio Historical Society; *Richard A. Pohrt; Phyllis Rabineau,* Custodian of Collections, Department of Anthropology, Field Museum of Natural History; *William C. Sturtevant,* Curator of North American Ethnology, Smithsonian Institution; *Judy Thompson,* Cataloguer, Canadian Ethnology Service; *David J. Wanger; Joe Ben Wheat,* Curator, University of Colorado Museum; *Hilary Caws;* and especially the helpful cooperation of *Vincent Wilcox,* Curator of North American Archaeology and Ethnology, Museum of the American Indian

Front cover illustration: False Face mask, Iroquois, wood, horsehair and tin, New York State Museum and Science Service, photograph by Alfred Tamarin. *Back cover illustration:* Bandolier bag, Chippewa, beads on cloth, University of Colorado Museum, photograph by Alfred Tamarin.

Macmillan Publishing Co., Inc., 866 Third Avenue, New York, N.Y. 10022
Collier Macmillan Canada, Ltd.
Printed in the United States of America

1 2 3 4 5 6 7 8 9 10

LIBRARY OF CONGRESS CATALOGING IN PUBLICATION DATA
Glubok, Shirley.   The art of the Woodland Indians.
SUMMARY: A survey of the art and crafts of the forest-dwelling Indians of the northern Atlantic seaboard and Great Lakes region. 1. Indians of North America—Art—Juvenile literature. 2. Indians of North America—Industries—Juvenile literature. [1. Indians of North America—Art. 2. Indians of North America—Industries] I. Title.
E98.A7G56   709'.01'1   76–12434   ISBN 0–02–736440–2

Handle on corn mush paddle, Iroquois, wood, Milwaukee Public Museum

When early explorers and settlers arrived on the eastern shores of what is now the United States and Canada, the land was covered with forests of maple, birch, oak, hickory, ash, elm, beech, pine and spruce. Plant life flourished, with an abundance of berry bushes and shrubs. The beautiful green woods teemed with animals, and turkeys, geese, wild ducks and other birds abounded. Clear lakes and streams were filled with fish.

The people who occupied the northeastern forests were members of various groups, each of which spoke a language belonging to one of three language families—Algonquian, Iroquoian and Siouan. Because they were all forest dwellers, they became known as the Woodland Indians.

The Woodlands covered a vast area that stretched along the Atlantic seaboard from what is now the upper part of North Carolina to the Canadian provinces of Nova Scotia and New Brunswick. Westward it extended across the northern shores of the Great Lakes to the rivers and streams that form the source of the Mississippi River, and southward beyond the Ohio River to the Appalachian Mountains.

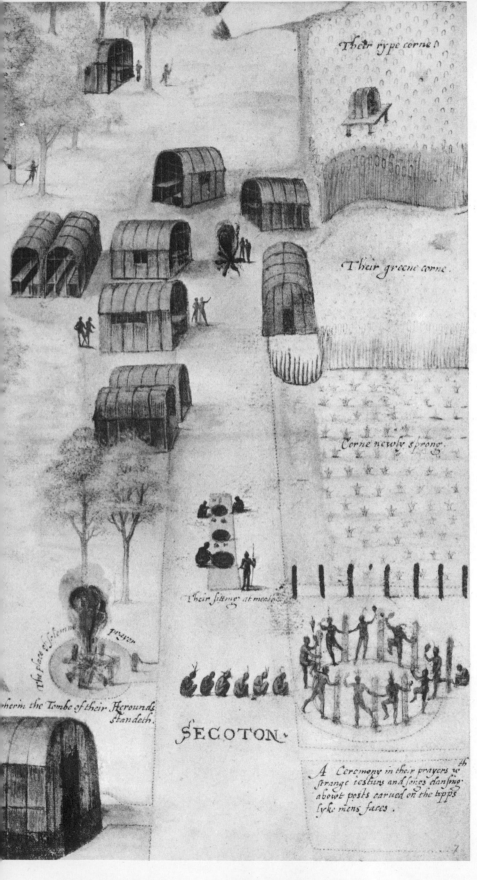

Their rype corne.

Their greene corne.

Corne newly sprong.

Their sitting at meate.

The place of solemne prayer.

herin the Tombe of their Herounds standeth.

SECOTON.

A Ceremony in their prayers w strange testures and songs danfing abowt posts carued on the topps lyke mens faces.

7

The first English colonists in America, who were sent out by Sir Walter Raleigh, landed in 1585 in what is now the state of North Carolina. They were met by an Algonquian people called the Secotan.

The Secotan lived in rectangular wigwams with rounded roofs. The framework was formed from the trunks of saplings, or young trees, that were cut down and set upright into the ground, then bent over at the top and tied together. The sides and roof were covered with bark or with mats made of thatch from plants that grow in the wetlands.

John White, whom Raleigh sent as governor of the colony in 1587, was an artist who made careful watercolors of these Algonquian Indians and their way of life. The picture at left shows their village and gardens with people feasting, dancing and hunting. The Woodland Indians lived mostly by hunting and fishing,

About 1585–1587,
British Museum

but they grew a few crops, especially corn, beans and squash, which they called "the three sisters."

The chief at right, painted by White, wears only a deerskin apron-skirt, with edges cut into fringes and an animal's tail dangling. In colder areas a man would wear a breechcloth and leggings that covered the entire leg. The people wore pearls or bone or shell beads as necklaces and earrings and sometimes wore feathers in their hair. They decorated their faces and bodies with paint or tattooing.

White made a trip back to England. When he returned in 1590 his colony had disappeared, without a trace except for the word "Croatan" carved into a tree. The English did not establish a permanent settlement until 1607 at Jamestown, Virginia, in the region of the Powhatan Indian Confederacy.

About 1585–1587,
British Museum

Explorers and fur trappers who traveled westward in the seventeenth century were astonished to find huge man-made mounds of earth in the Ohio River valley. Some of the mounds were 70 feet high and measured 900 feet around. Most of the earthworks covered the graves of prehistoric Indians.

The earliest of the mound builders lived in the Ohio River valley 2,500 years ago. They became known as the Adena because several of their burial mounds were found on property belonging to a man by that name.

The Adena lived in cone-shaped huts made of bark. They hunted with spears, gathered wild foods, fished and grew some squash, sunflowers and pumpkins, and perhaps even a little corn.

When an important person died, elaborate funeral ceremonies were held. Works of art were buried with him and an earth mound was built over the grave. The human form at left is a tubular pipe, carved from Ohio soapstone, that was found in an

Adena mound. An opening for the smoke was hollowed out from head to toe in the figure. The bowl for the tobacco is in the base, between the feet; the mouthpiece is on top of the head.

The Adena culture lasted around six hundred years, until new people came into the area. They are called Hopewell because a group of their mounds was found on a farm by that name. The pipe in the form of a duck perched on top of a fish was made by a Hopewell carver. The back of the duck is hollowed out to form the bowl of the pipe. Smoke could be drawn in through a narrow opening in the fish. Elaborate pipes were probably smoked in ceremonies.

The Hopewell lived by hunting animals for meat and gathering wild food. They also planted some corn in small gardens. The people wore clothing made of animal skins, fur or fabric woven from tree bark or plant stems.

Field Museum of Natural History, Chicago

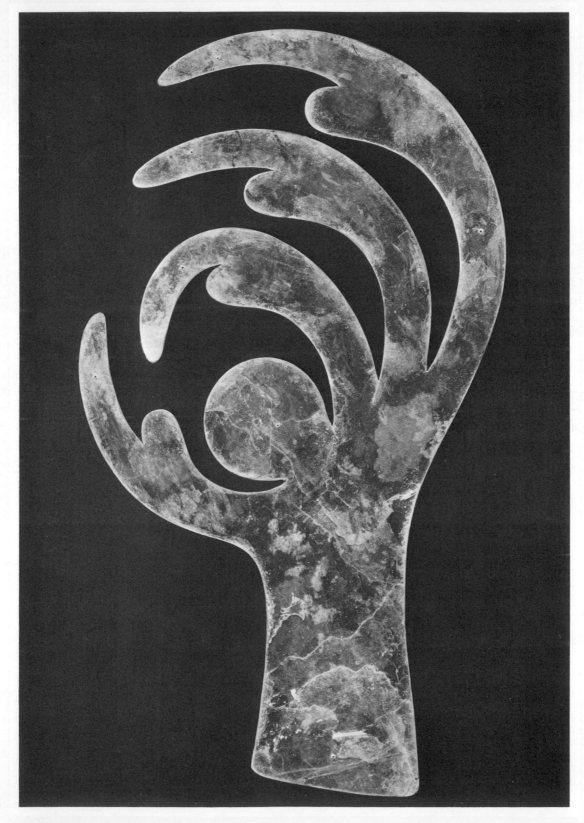

The object at left in the form of a claw may have been connected with Hopewell burial ceremonies. It was cut out of mica, a thin silvery mineral from the Appalachian Mountains.

Beautifully decorated pottery vessels were also buried with the dead. Hopewell potters ground up soft rock and mixed it with clay to prevent the vessels from cracking as they were fired, or baked. The pots were made by molding a base, then winding coils of clay to form the sides. The coils were smoothed by beating the walls of the vessel with a wooden paddle. The clay figure of a mother and child at right, found in a mound in Illinois, was also made by the Hopewell.

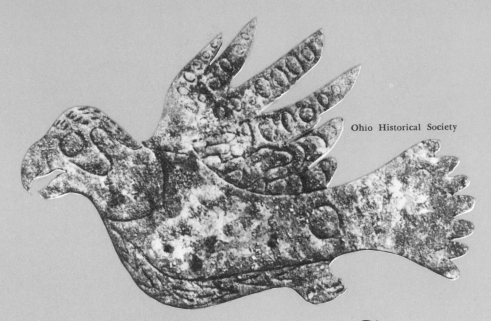

*T*he copper ornament in the form of a bird, above, was buried in a Hopewell mound in Ohio. To make the ornament, lumps of copper were beaten into a thin sheet and the figure was cut out with stone tools.

Stone tools were also used to chip away the edges of pieces of flint or other hard rock to make spearheads for hunting. At left is a Hopewell flint spear point.

Spear throwers, called atlatls, increased the throwing power of a hunter's arm. Winglike objects of polished stone with holes in the center, called bannerstones, are thought to have been used as

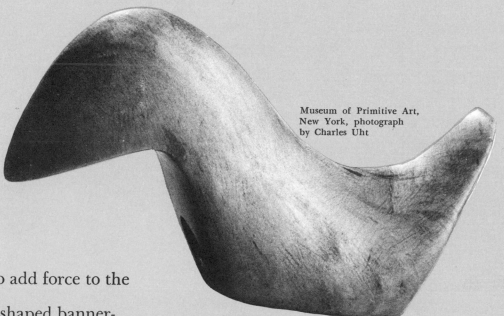

handles or weights on the atlatl to add force to the thrust of the spear. The butterfly-shaped banner-stone at right is made of banded slate.

Polished stone objects in the shape of birds, called birdstones, may have had the same purpose. A bannerstone or birdstone was made by chipping a piece of stone into the rough shape of the object, then polishing it by rubbing with fine sandstone. Holes could be made by placing sand where the opening was to be bored and turning a stick on that spot. Birdstones and bannerstones have been found throughout the Woodlands. It is not known who made these two, nor when they were made.

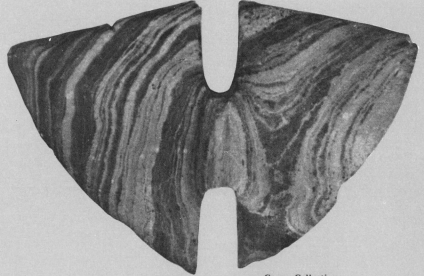

A View Near Point Levy Opposite Quebec, by Thomas Davies, 1788, The National Gallery of Canada, Ottawa

The first Americans to be seen by Europeans were probably the ancestors of the Micmac of eastern Canada, whom the Norsemen came upon when they landed in North America around a thousand years ago. About five hundred years later an Italian navigator, John Cabot, also saw these people when he was exploring the North American continent under the British flag in 1497.

The name Micmac means "allies," but their neighbors, the Malecite, called them by a name meaning "porcupine Indians" because the Micmac were skilled in making decorations with porcupine quills. The scene at left shows a Micmac settlement. People are wearing a mixture of European-style and typical Micmac clothing.

In winter these people were forest hunters, chasing moose, caribou and porcupine. In summer they fished along the coast. The Micmac lived in cone-shaped wigwams made of a framework of saplings set in a circle. The saplings were tied together at the top and the framework was covered with birchbark. Bark from the birch tree is wind and water-proof, light yet flexible. It grows in layers of different thickness and is removed from the trees most easily in summer.

Birchbark was used to make this Micmac model canoe decorated with porcupine quills. To make a canoe, the bark was stretched over a light framework of wooden ribs and sewn with roots from a tree. The seams were filled in with pine pitch or spruce gum. Micmac canoes were streamlined to move rapidly through the water and were light enough for portaging, or being carried over land from one body of water to another.

The Micmac were also skilled at making toboggans and snowshoes.

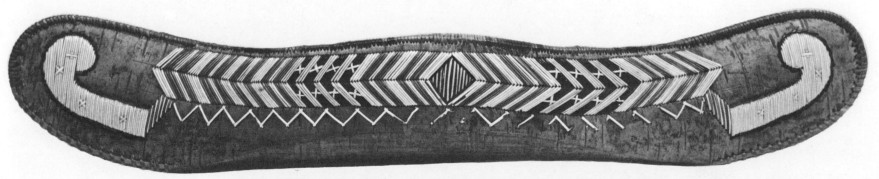

Canadian Ethnology Service, National Museum of Man, National Museums of Canada, Ottawa

Chippewa Mode of Traveling in Winter, by Peter Rindisbacher, about 1833, The West Point Museum, U.S. Military Academy

Shoes that permit a person to walk on the surface of deep snow were an Indian invention. Snowshoes were useful for chasing large animals in winter. The animals would sink into snow drifts, and hunters wearing snowshoes could close in for the kill. Snowshoes were made by stretching webs of babiches, thongs made from the skin or muscle of the moose or caribou, over a wooden frame. A Chippewa, or Ojibwa, Indian wearing snowshoes leads his family on a winter journey, at left. The same people are called Chippewa in the United States and Ojibwa in Canada. Both names come from an Indian word referring to the puckered seams in their moccasins. The family's dogs are pulling a toboggan, another Indian invention. "Toboggan" is an Algonquian word that has been adopted into the English language.

A Chippewa woman made the designs in birchbark, below, with her teeth. She folded a thin strip of bark and bit through the layers to make tiny holes, then unfolded the strip to reveal the repeated patterns.

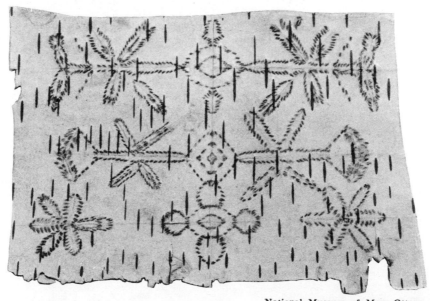

National Museum of Man, Ottawa,
photograph by Alfred Tamarin

When Woodland people wanted a permanent record of an important event, they wove pictures and symbols into wide beaded bands called wampum belts. Below is the Hiawatha Belt, a record of the formation of the Iroquois League of Five Nations in 1570. According to legend, Hiawatha formed the League with Deganawidah, who crossed Lake Ontario in a great white stone canoe. To help Hiawatha cross the lake, ducks lifted up the water so he could walk with dry moccasins. Deganawidah and Hiawatha called the chiefs together beneath the Evergrowing Tree of Peace, an enormous white pine. The League of Five Nations was made up of the Mohawk, Oneida, Onondaga, Cayuga and Seneca. Later they were joined by the Tuscarora and became the Six Nations.

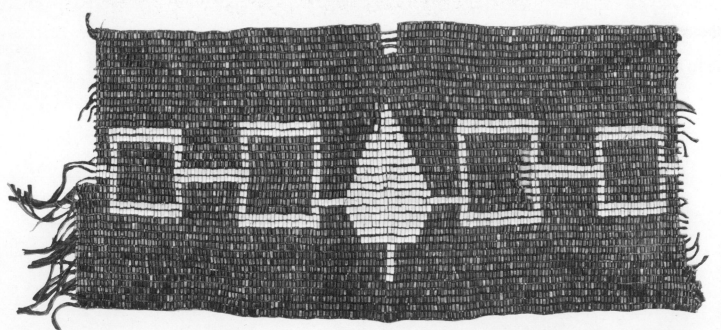

New York State Museum and Science Service, Albany

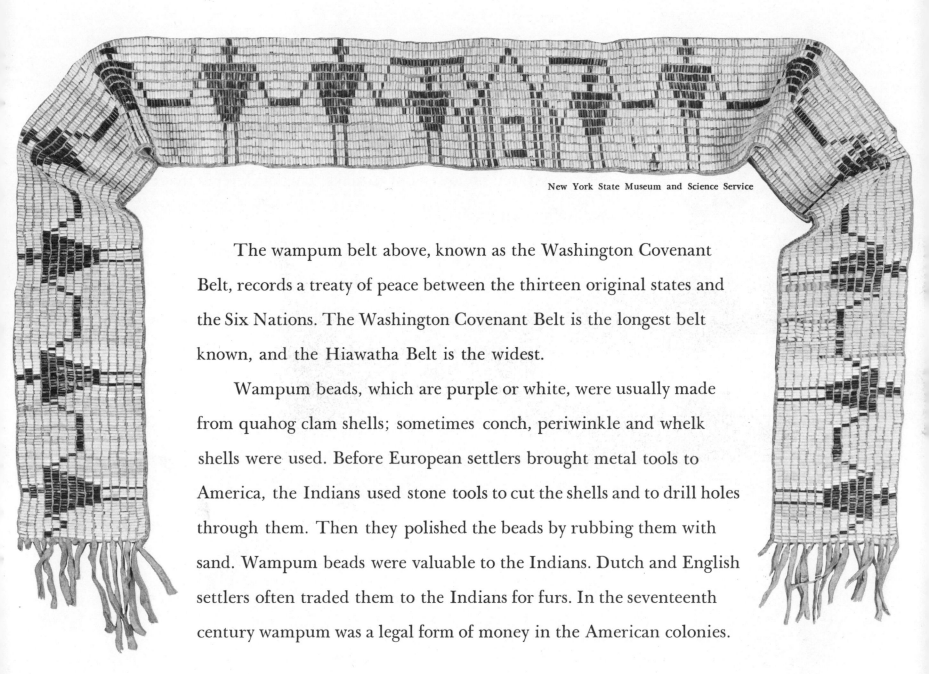

The wampum belt above, known as the Washington Covenant Belt, records a treaty of peace between the thirteen original states and the Six Nations. The Washington Covenant Belt is the longest belt known, and the Hiawatha Belt is the widest.

Wampum beads, which are purple or white, were usually made from quahog clam shells; sometimes conch, periwinkle and whelk shells were used. Before European settlers brought metal tools to America, the Indians used stone tools to cut the shells and to drill holes through them. Then they polished the beads by rubbing them with sand. Wampum beads were valuable to the Indians. Dutch and English settlers often traded them to the Indians for furs. In the seventeenth century wampum was a legal form of money in the American colonies.

ampum beads were also worn as decoration. This doll made by the Huron Indians is wearing a wampum necklace and carrying a tomahawk, or war hatchet, with a metal blade. The handles of these hatchets were often hollowed out to make tomahawk pipes that could be used for smoking tobacco.

Before metal was available, war clubs, called pogamoggans, were carved from a single piece of heavy wood. The weapons have round heads and long curved handles. The maple war club at far right has a knob carved from a burl, or knot, on a tree. The animal head at the tip of the handle may represent the owner's clan. A clan is a group of families that claim to be descended from the same ancestor. Animals would be adopted by a clan so that their spirits would act as protectors, and figures of the animals became clan symbols.

The club was found in Pennsylvania. It probably belonged to an Iroquois warrior who took part in the defeat of the British general Sir Edward Braddock during the French and Indian War. The war was fought between England and France on American soil from 1755 to 1763; Indians allied themselves with both sides. War clubs were used in hand-to-hand fighting. When Europeans brought metal blades to make tomahawks, wooden war clubs continued to be used for ceremonial purposes. A Chippewa war dance is represented below.

Denver Art Museum, photograph by Alfred Tamarin

By George Catlin, 1855, Collection of Richard A. Pohrt, Jr., photograph by Alfred Tamarin

Canadian Ethnology Service,
National Museum of Man,
National Museums of Canada

When firearms became available to the Woodland Indians, loose grains of gun-powder were kept in containers of animal horn. The powder was poured from the horn into the muzzle end of the gun and then the shot was rammed in. Above is a powder horn attached to a woven sash which was worn over the shoulder. The sash was finger-woven of wool yarn by Algonquian Indians in the Great Lakes region. In finger-weaving a single set of threads is hung on a short stick and woven together by braiding.

The Chippewa sash, above right, is interwoven with beads in a diagonal, or slanting, pattern. Porcupine quills are worked into the weave in a vertical pattern and are also wrapped around the fringes. Sashes were worn around the waist, over the shoulder or wrapped around the head as a turban. Before the Indians obtained wool yarn from traders, they made sashes from animal hair or natural fibers from plants such as nettle or basswood.

Joseph Brant, or Thayendanegea, a Mohawk, is shown below wearing a sash over his shoulder and a powder horn. Brant

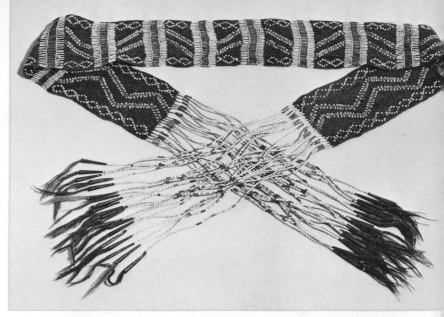

By William Berczy, about 1805–1807,
The National Gallery of Canada

sided with the British in the Revolutionary War and twice visited England. When the British lost the war, he went to Canada to live.

In the portrait he is wearing a European-style cloth shirt and woolen blanket. Before wool became available, furs and animal hides were worn as blankets. His arm bands and the silver medallion around his neck were probably gifts, but his moccasins, leggings and splendid garters are Indian-made. Underneath Brant's powder horn is a skin pouch to hold shot for his gun.

*E*very Indian who carried a gun wore a pouch over his shoulder. It served as a container for his gunshot and his strike-a-light kit, a piece of flint and steel to produce sparks for making fire. The Iroquois skin pouch at left was dyed black, and a design of thunderbirds was sewn on with porcupine quills. The bag was once owned by Sir Jeffrey Amherst, an English general who served in the American colonies during the French and Indian War.

When manufactured cloth and glass beads were obtained from the Europeans, the Indians used them to decorate large bandolier bags. Bandoliers were mainly for display, and several of them might be worn at the same time. Some were called "friendship bags" because men would load them with gifts when they went visiting.

The Chippewa bag at near right has geometric designs that were woven on a box-shaped wooden loom with threads attached from end to end. The solid beadwork on the Chippewa bag at far right was sewn onto the cloth. In the northern Woodlands, French nuns who instructed Indian girls in sewing used leaf and flower embroidery designs.

Tobacco bags, or fire bags, held pipes and smoking equipment. The beaded fire bag in the center, below, was made by the Micmac for the Duke of Kent, a member of the British royal family. The Indians were the first people ever to grow tobacco plants for smoking.

Denver Art Museum,
photograph by Alfred Tamarin

McCord Museum, Montreal,
photograph by Alfred Tamarin

Denver Art Museum,
photograph by Alfred Tamarin

23

According to a Menomini legend, tobacco was given to the Indians by the hero Nanabush, who smelled the smoke and asked a mountain giant to give him some. When the giant refused, Nanabush stole some bags full of tobacco and ran off, pursued by the giant. By trickery Nanabush threw the giant down and foretold that he would turn into a grasshopper and shoot tobacco juice from his mouth.

At Indian councils before a meeting began or a treaty was agreed on, it was the custom to pass a pipe to all present. The stone pipe above was carved by Awbonwaishkum, an Ottawa chief, in the mid-nineteenth century. The chair, on which one of the figures is seated, was unknown to the Indians before the arrival of Europeans in America.

Awbonwaishkum used an old knife and a broken file to carve his pipe.

At right is a wooden heddle, which kept the threads separate when weaving beaded bands. Each of the warp threads, the lengthwise threads in weaving, went through a hole in the center of the heddle. It was carved by a Fox Indian, John Young Bear. The names of Indian carvers are usually unknown.

Curved knives, called "crooked knives," were useful for woodworking. The metal blades were made from steel files or knives obtained through trade. The horsehead handle on this Chippewa crooked knife was carved from curly maple.

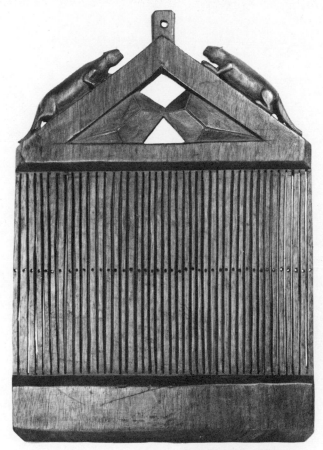

Chandler-Pohrt Collection

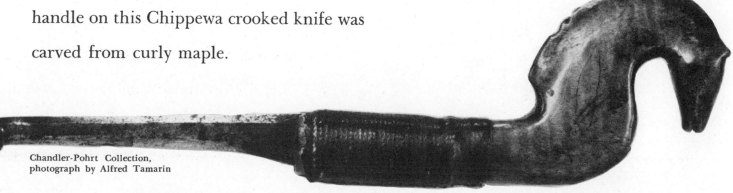

Chandler-Pohrt Collection,
photograph by Alfred Tamarin

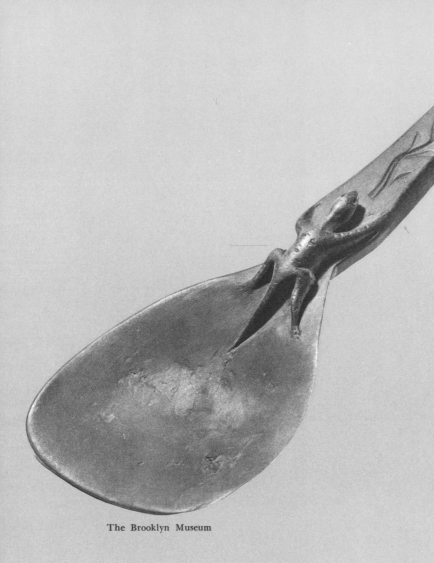

The Brooklyn Museum

Denver Art Museum,
photograph by Alfred Tamarin

Among the Woodland Indians, the charring and scraping method was used to make wooden bowls, spoons and dugout canoes. To hollow them out, the Indians burned the wood, then scraped away the ash with bone and stone tools. Final carving might be done with a beaver tooth attached to a wooden handle. In later times crooked knives made the work easier.

When Indian people were invited to a feast, each person carried his own wooden bowl and spoon. A salamander, probably a clan animal, was carved on the Ottawa spoon above left. Its curved handle would fit over the edge of a bowl.

The small Winnebago bowl at left was made from a burl. Before metal tools were available, burls were split from trees with wedges of deer antler. This bowl, with a human head on its rim,

was used for mixing herbs and other plants in the preparation of medicine. The natural grain of the wood makes an interesting pattern. Larger bowls were used for mixing dough for corn bread or for serving and eating food. Pioneers in America often used Indian-made bowls.

The Iroquois made fine pots. The lines in the designs were formed in the soft clay before the pots were fired. When Europeans began trading iron and copper kettles for Indian goods, especially for the fur of the beaver, the Iroquois stopped making clay vessels.

Gourds were often used as containers for food and water. In John White's watercolor at right, the woman is carrying a jar made out of a hollow gourd. The child's doll was probably given to her by one of the settlers.

1585–1587, British Museum

A Micmac made the round box above out of bark from the birch tree and decorated it with porcupine quills. Holes were punched in the birchbark with a pointed tool called an awl, and the quills were inserted. Before traders brought metal, awls were made of animal bones.

Splints, or thin strips of wood, usually ash or white oak, are used for weaving beautiful baskets even to this day. The splints come from layers of wood that have been loosened by beating the trunk of a tree that has been felled. A splint gauge, a tool with sharp metal blades, cuts and separates the splints into narrow strips, which are woven into baskets.

The Iroquois basket at right is decorated with stamped designs, using paints made from berries. Stamps were made from a variety of things, including carved wood or raw potatoes.

National Museum of Man, Ottawa, photograph by Alfred Tamarin

The Sauk and Fox bag, below right, was woven from the inner bark of the basswood tree. Before weaving, the bark was dyed with the juice of berries and other plants. The Potawatomi bag for storing medicine, below left, was also woven from natural plant materials. The design represents an underwater panther, a tremendous creature with a long tail, horns and snakelike skin. This mythical panther lives underwater but moves freely over land. The creature has knowledge of plants that can cure disease and prolong or shorten life, which gives him power over birds, animals and men.

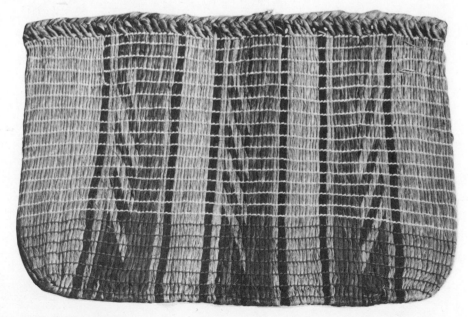

Field Museum of Natural History, photographs by Alfred Tamarin

*W*oodland Indians wore soft-soled moccasins made from buckskin. Each tribe had a slightly different style. The imprint of a moccasin in the earth could reveal the tribe that made it. Moccasins are flexible and warm and can be comfortably worn with snowshoes.

The moccasin at left has upright ankle flaps, typical of the Huron. The skin was dyed black and decorated with moose hair embroidery. Hairs from the mane, cheeks and rump of a moose are long and can be easily

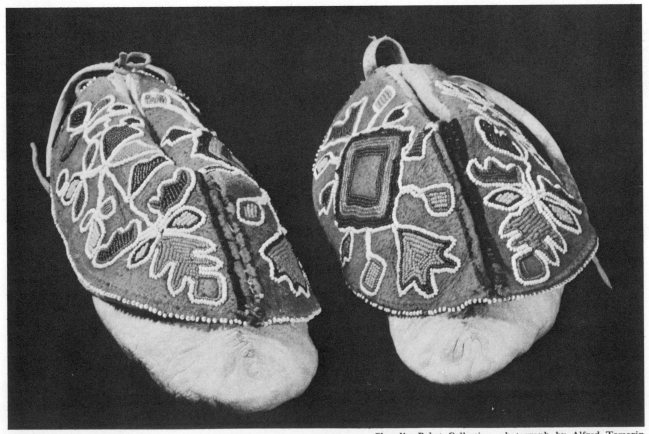

dyed. Along the lower edge of the embroidery is a row of metal cones fringed with animal hair.

On the Potawatomi moccasins, below left, beads are sewn onto the wide cuffs that turn down over the foot. Two different designs are on each cuff, one on the inside and one on the outside of the foot.

The Winnebago also wore moccasins with wide cuffs. The doll at right is dressed like a stylish Winnebago woman. She wears a long skirt sewn with ribbonwork designs. Woodland Indian women admired the French silk ribbons brought by traders and used them to decorate clothing. Pieces of ribbon were cut out and sewn down with silk thread in beautiful designs. The patterns, made of bark, paper or cardboard, were often handed down from mother to daughter. Ribbonwork from a Menomini skirt is shown below. The Menomini harvested wild rice, which was so important to them that they are known as the "wild rice people." Even today each family gives thanks when they eat the new crop.

Denver Art Museum,
photograph by Alfred Tamarin

National Museum of Man, Ottawa, photograph by Alfred Tamarin

31

*R*ibbonwork decorates the miniature blanket
that wraps this Micmac papoose doll snugly on
its cradleboard. "Papoose," the general word for
an Indian baby, comes from the language of
Indians in New England, as does "squaw," the word
for woman. Roger Williams, who lived among the
Narragansett, was the first to record these words.
Williams founded the colony of Rhode Island.

Woodland Indian mothers are loving to their

babies and treat them gently. A papoose would be bound to a flat board and carried on the mother's back all day. And it was easy to hang the cradleboard in a tree or to lean it against the wigwam. A hoop protected the baby in case the cradleboard should fall; toys could be attached to it to amuse the child. The back of a Mohawk cradleboard at far left is carved and painted with floral designs.

Cradleboards were often decorated with panels of quillwork designs. The Chippewa cradleboard strap below was made by wrapping quills around thongs of skin, then weaving them into designs. The winged figures represent the mythical thunderbird whose eyes flash lightning and whose wings beat thunder. It constantly battles against underground forces and can bring man victory in war.

Quillwork is an ancient art among Woodland Indians. The quills were soaked to soften them, then flattened and dyed before they were wrapped, woven or sewn.

Canadian Ethnology Service, National Museum of Man, National Museums of Canada

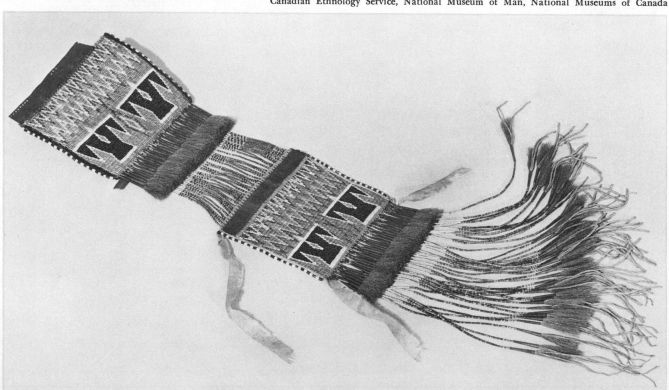

As part of their Midwinter Festival, Iroquois dancers wearing False Face masks enter the houses of their neighbors and scatter hot ashes on people to prevent illness during the coming year. If they come upon somebody already ill, they dance, shaking rattles, and pray to help him recover.

Ceremonies are held in the Long House, the sacred structure of the Iroquois, where prayers of thanksgiving are said and medicine societies hold dances and act out dreams. Tobacco is burned to the spirits, and legends about the False Faces are told.

Crane Collection,
Denver Museum of Natural History,
photographs by Alfred Tamarin

False Face masks to be worn in the dances are carved by those who saw the faces in dreams. The carving is begun in a living tree, usually basswood. The carver burns tobacco and prays to the spirit of the tree, asking the spirit to give curing powers to the wearer of the mask. He cuts out the rough features of the mask before removing it from the tree to finish the carving, then paints it. If the mask is cut away from the tree in the morning, it is painted red. If removed in the afternoon, the mask is painted black. The mask in the tree at right was carved by Chief Grey Cloud of the Cayuga.

The masks represent friendly spirits who are supposed to frighten away evil spirits. The doll made of corn husks at far left is wearing a False Face mask with a whistling mouth. The doll near left and the mask in the tree represent Old Broken Nose.

An Iroquois legend relates that the Creator of All Good Things made the earth, then

Photograph by Alfred Tamarin

traveled about on it. He met Hadui, the Great Humpback, a giant who carries an entire tree as his staff and shakes the earth as he walks. When Hadui boasted, "I am the master of creation," the Creator challenged him to a test of strength to see who could move mountains. Hadui shook his huge turtle rattle; the earth trembled and a mountain moved partly toward him. Then the Creator summoned a mountain. When Hadui turned suddenly and smashed his face on the mountainside, he admitted that the Creator was "master of all." Hadui appears as Old Broken Nose, with a bent nose and crooked mouth, carrying his staff and shaking his rattle to chase away illness and calm storms.

New York State Museum
and Science Service,
photograph by Alfred Tamarin

The mask at far left, with protruding lips, is a Doorkeeper. The one at near left, made by an Onondaga, is a Pipe Mouth which blows smoke through its mouth in the dances. The laughing Beggar mask at right was worn by small boys when they went around begging for tobacco for the Midwinter Festival.

Eyes of False Faces are usually rimmed with tin or copper, and the masks are trimmed with horsehair. Pouches of tobacco are tied to them when they are blessed to make them sacred.

New York State Museum and Science Service,
photographs by Alfred Tamarin

Crane Collection,
Denver Museum of Natural History,
photograph by Alfred Tamarin

*H*usk Face messengers, who also have powers to cure, race through the community ahead of the False Face dancers. They represent agricultural spirits who taught the Iroquois to grow crops and to hunt. The spirits inhabit a valley on the other side of the earth, and they come at Midwinter to help the people.

Husk Face masks are made by drying corn husks, cutting them into strips and braiding them, then winding the braids into coils and sewing them together. The sections around each eye and the mouth are coiled separately. Additional rows of coils are wound entirely around the face with strips of corn husk forming a fringe. At left is a corn husk doll wearing a Husk Face mask. The mask at right, with a long corn husk nose, represents a woman.

*A*mong the Great Lakes Indians, the Grand Medicine Society, or Midéwiwin, performs dance ceremonies to cure the sick and renew life. The members, both men and women, sing magic songs and shake rattles. The ceremonies are so long and complicated that it is difficult to remember the order of the songs and dances. To be sure no mistakes are made, memory guides showing the order of events for all of the participants are engraved on a scroll or roll of birchbark. The scrolls also show how the ceremonial objects should be arranged.

Wooden plaques with engraved picture writing help the singers to remember the order of their own magic songs. The Chippewa song record above was used as the top of a box in which feathers were stored between ceremonies.

Midéwiwin members keep their medicine objects in bags made of a whole otter skin. To the Indian, "medicine" means more than remedies to cure the sick; medicine is believed to give its owner special powers which can help friends or harm enemies. The tail and paws on the Chippewa otter skin bag, far left, are covered with cloth sewn with beadwork designs. The dangling tassels are made out of thimbles.

Below left is a Chippewa cloth bag worn by a singer in the Midéwiwin ceremonies. The horned figure outlined in beads represents a horrible creature that eats human flesh. The songs sung are legends of the history and migration of the people.

Midéwiwin leaders sometimes perform magic with little wooden figures. The Menomini juggler dolls, below right, are attached to wands so that they can be moved about during the ceremonies.

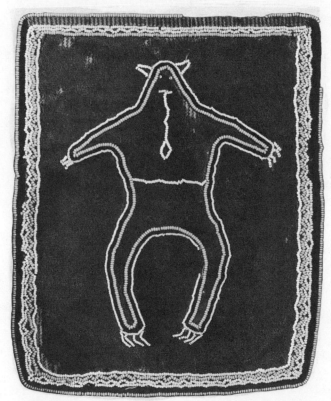

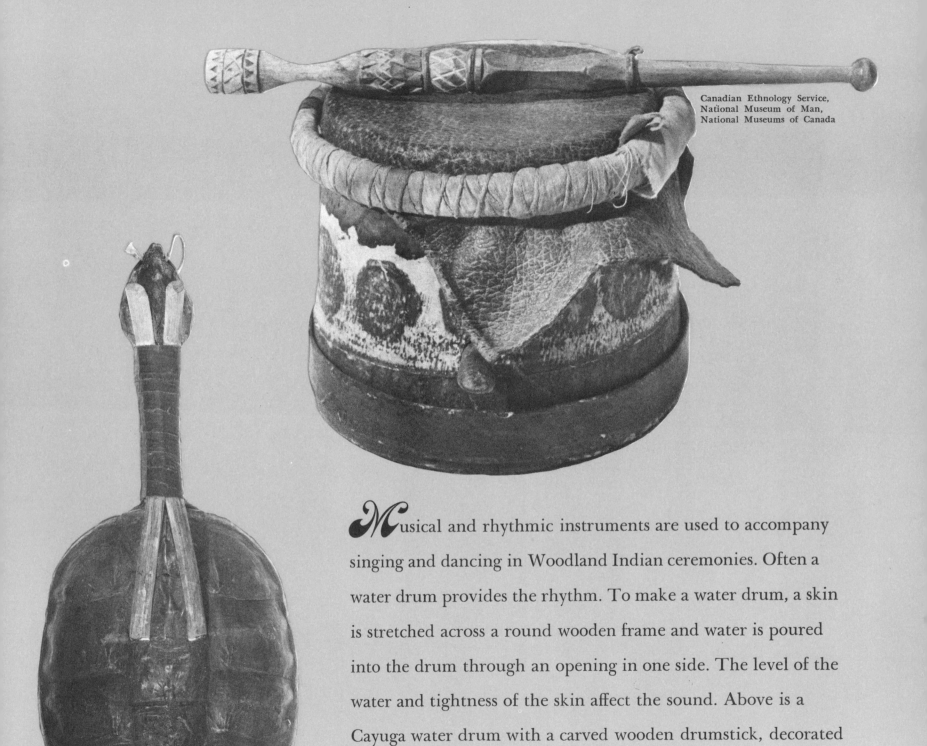

Canadian Ethnology Service,
National Museum of Man,
National Museums of Canada

Milwaukee Public Museum

Musical and rhythmic instruments are used to accompany singing and dancing in Woodland Indian ceremonies. Often a water drum provides the rhythm. To make a water drum, a skin is stretched across a round wooden frame and water is poured into the drum through an opening in one side. The level of the water and tightness of the skin affect the sound. Above is a Cayuga water drum with a carved wooden drumstick, decorated with painted designs.

Turtle shell rattles are used in ceremonies of the Iroquois

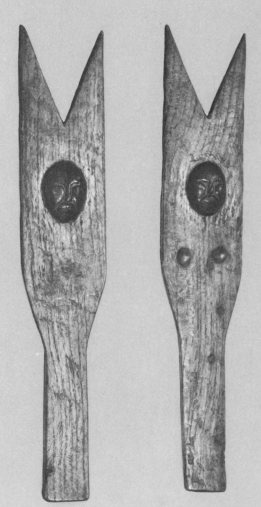

False Face Society. Quartz pebbles, corn kernels or even cherry pits are placed inside the empty shell of a turtle. The handle is made with splints of wood, wrapped with strips of skin, that secure the turtle's head at the end.

An Iroquois legend relates that when the world was being formed the Great Turtle offered its back to support the floating earth. There is another legend that the turtle gave man fire.

The drumsticks at left, carved with faces representing a male and female spirit, were used during the Big House Ceremony, the most important religious event among the Delaware Indians.

To woo their brides, young men played music on flutes. Young women were not permitted to leave their homes when a flute was being played, but the songs carried so well that a girl could be serenaded from afar. Tiny horses' heads are carved on the Menomini flute, above.

By George Catlin, about 1832, Field Museum of Natural History

Denver Art Museum, photograph by Alfred Tamarin

Indian warriors of the Woodlands wore roaches, crests of long animal hair. Sauk and Fox warriors removed most of the hair from their heads and left only a scalp lock on top, which was tied to the roach. Black Hawk, a famous Sauk chief, is wearing a roach in the portrait at left. This chief bravely resisted the advance of white settlers, saying that the Great Spirit had given the land to His children to live on. In 1832 he led his men against American troops in what came to be known as the Black Hawk War. As a result of this war, the Sauk and Fox were nearly wiped out. They had to give up their immense areas of land in Michigan, Wisconsin and Illinois and move west of the Mississippi River. In the portrait Black Hawk is holding a calumet, or medicine pipe, decorated with a bird and feathers.

A Menomini roach of dyed deer hair is shown at left, below. A roach spreader of bone, antler or silver would be inserted in the center of the headdress to push the hairs outward so that the roach would stand up.

Woodland Indians admired the silver jewelry that was worn by early settlers. They began to wear European jewelry, and then they learned to make their own. At first they hammered it out of silver coins. Then they began to use German silver, which is a combination of nickel, zinc and copper.

Round brooches were popular as decorations on women's dresses. An Abnaki silver brooch can be seen above. A beautiful Menomini Indian girl wears a blouse covered with silver brooches in the portrait at right. The brooches are a sign of wealth. Only a rich person could afford to wear so much silver.

Milwaukee Public Museum

Ke-wah-ten or The North Wind,
by Paul Kane, about 1845,
Stark Museum of Art, Orange, Texas

Sault Ste. Marie, by Paul Kane, about 1845–1848, Royal Ontario Museum

In the Great Lakes region the Chippewa lived in round wigwams made of birchbark. Mats woven of bullrushes were stretched over the lower part, and the dome was made of overlapping layers of birchbark which had been stripped from the trees in large pieces and sewn together with long roots. Often poles were fastened to the outside to keep the bark in place. An opening was left for the door and a hole in the roof allowed the smoke of the fire to escape. These houses were portable, as the bark and rush mats could be carried in bundles.

The people in the center of the painting above are preparing food in a large birchbark container. These vessels could be made watertight by sealing the seams with spruce gum or pitch. They had many uses as dishes, buckets and containers for cooking and storing. To cook in a birchbark container, it was filled with water and heated stones were dropped into it.

Birchbark vessels were often decorated by scraping away the outer layer of the bark to create designs. Below is a Chippewa "mokuk," which has a round top and flat sides that are wider at the bottom. To make a mokuk, the bark was cut and then folded. The sides were sewn together and a hoop was sewn to the top by piercing holes in the bark and inserting cedar roots with a bone needle. Mokuks were used for carrying and storing berries, wild rice or maple sugar.

A legend tells how the Indians got maple sugar. One day Wenebojo, grandson of the earth, was standing under a tree when it began to rain maple syrup. He held out a birchbark container to catch the sugary rain. Wenebojo thought that maple syrup falling from the sky was too easy for the Indians to collect. He decided that they would have to pray to the spirits for it, making offerings of tobacco to them. Then he taught the Indians to collect maple sap by tapping the tree and inserting a wooden wedge so the sap would flow into a container.

Royal Ontario Museum

*T*oday a number of Indian artists are expressing traditional ideas in terms of modern art. Saul Williams, a Chippewa, used commercial paint and paper for *Nanabush*, at right. According to legend, Nanabush could change to whatever form he wished at any time. To help animals, he became an animal himself. In order to help man, he became a man.

The early European explorers and settlers arrived in the Woodlands carrying iron tools and armed with muskets and gunpowder. They found themselves among people who used tools of bone or stone, and fought back with bows and arrows.

Royal Ontario Museum

It was an unequal struggle for the Native Americans. But though their homelands were quickly overrun by incoming settlers, the Indians of the Woodlands were never completely driven away. From Maine and eastern Canada to the Carolinas, they still live near the lands of their ancestors. For example, many of the Iroquois in New York State still worship in their traditional Long Houses and practice their native arts. Despite the pressures of colonization, war, famine and disease, the Indians of the Woodlands have not vanished.

Other books by Shirley Glubok:

THE ART OF ANCIENT EGYPT
THE ART OF LANDS IN THE BIBLE
THE ART OF THE NORTH AMERICAN INDIAN
THE ART OF THE ESKIMO
THE ART OF ANCIENT GREECE
THE ART OF ANCIENT ROME
THE ART OF AFRICA
ART AND ARCHAEOLOGY
THE ART OF ANCIENT PERU
THE ART OF THE ETRUSCANS
THE ART OF ANCIENT MEXICO
KNIGHTS IN ARMOR
THE ART OF INDIA
THE ART OF JAPAN
THE ART OF COLONIAL AMERICA
THE ART OF THE SOUTHWEST INDIANS
THE ART OF THE OLD WEST
THE ART OF THE NEW AMERICAN NATION
THE ART OF THE SPANISH IN THE UNITED STATES
AND PUERTO RICO
THE ART OF CHINA
THE ART OF AMERICA FROM JACKSON TO LINCOLN
THE ART OF AMERICA IN THE GILDED AGE
THE ART OF AMERICA IN THE EARLY
TWENTIETH CENTURY
THE ART OF AMERICA SINCE WORLD WAR II
THE ART OF THE NORTHWEST COAST INDIANS
THE ART OF THE PLAINS INDIANS
THE FALL OF THE AZTECS
THE FALL OF THE INCAS
DISCOVERING TUT-ANKH-AMEN'S TOMB
DISCOVERING THE ROYAL TOMBS AT UR
DIGGING IN ASSYRIA
HOME AND CHILD LIFE IN COLONIAL DAYS
DOLLS DOLLS DOLLS

With Alfred Tamarin:

ANCIENT INDIANS OF THE SOUTHWEST
VOYAGING TO CATHAY: AMERICANS IN THE CHINA TRADE
OLYMPIC GAMES IN ANCIENT GREECE